A New Beginning
City of Philadelphia

Morgan Evans Maeves
On
The Issues

I0424689

Copyright © 2019 Morgan E. Maeves

All Rights Reserved

FOREWORD

"Persistence, perseverance must pervade in order to prevail." -Unknown

FOREWORD

"Persistence, perseverance must pervade in order to prevail." -Unknown

A New Beginning
City of Philadelphia

Morgan Evans Maeves
On
The Issues

Copyright © 2019 Morgan E. Maeves

TABLE OF CONTENTS

CHAPTER 1 – BACKGROUND

It's important to recognize that in 1776, the Founding Fathers intended that all private citizens be able to run for office in the community. When I look around the city, I see much promise and untapped potential. As the 5th largest U.S. city, we should not have a poverty rate of 25%. We must implement practical solutions to improve society and grant the most beneficial opportunities for our city's growth and its citizens. I grew up

A NEW BEGINNING

A NEW BEGINNING

in the city of Philadelphia as a young boy wondering what my future would hold. I know the meaning of hard work and having resilience since I come from a middle-class family. At the time I am writing this, I'm a 21-year-old young man who wants to advocate for the voiceless. I'd like to serve the community and be the catalyst for widespread change. What I lack in experience, I compensate for in ideas and vibrant energy as a citizen just like the rest of us. Career politicians have always given the same solutions which lead to the same results. As young people, we can change that

through ingenuity and thinking outside the

box. I consider myself a moderate and a

pragmatic populist, and I always think of

those who are less fortunate than myself and

families who are forced to live in poverty or

remain without shelter for prolonged periods

of time. In June 2018, as I walked through

Center City, I witnessed a horrendous sight.

On the sidewalks, there were people living in

squalor on a city porch. These are conditions

no Philadelphian should be subjected to

during their lives. Each person deserves

A NEW BEGINNING

adequate shelter and a place where they can be cared for and their needs met. It is important to be a visionary and seek a better direction for our city. As a student, I recognize that it can be an arduous task to ascend to top leadership positions. I believe that everything is possible, and that you can fulfill your dreams. Whatever they may be, we need to reach so far to achieve our fullest potential. It all starts with us; we must be willing to undertake challenges that no one else would ever think of taking on. I've always said that I would never run for a

A NEW BEGINNING

public role unless I felt that something needed to be rectified. Our city deserves leaders who will be responsible, effective managers, and someone who embraces diversity of all cultures and walks of life. I believe that my college education made me more well-rounded. It allows you to function as a productive citizen in your community and life. During the time I am writing this, I am still pursuing a major in public administration with minors in history and economics. I believe the choice of this major provided me with greater insight into the

A NEW BEGINNING

issues that plague inner cities. I've had a commitment to keep those who are less fortunate in mind and do everything I could to help them get the necessary assistance. Serving as an effective leader and representative requires you to listen to the needs and concerns of others, and not to do only what you want. A leader must answer to the people and strive to give them a better life. I've had several involvements that bolstered my leadership and decision-making abilities along with newfound skills in communication, organization, teamwork, and

A NEW BEGINNING

cooperation. I had the privilege to serve on student government and work to enact environmental reforms. In 2017, I helped implement sustainable solutions for my college campus. I believe this is excellent training for someone who desires to be a leader in our community. I served as a coordinator for an environmental group on my college campus as well. Despite us being a smaller organization composed of around 70 members total with only 10 active members, I rebuilt the organization. We must have more college students becoming involved in the community to revitalize situations. I encouraged others serving with me in leadership positions that I affirmed their potential and offered suggestions to improve their performance. When someone doesn't perform up to expectations, the last thing that they need is someone else telling them that they aren't good enough. I feel my university experiences have allowed me to grow and learn from mistakes to lead effectively. We all needed to come together to accomplish a mutual goal. This is important for any leader.

CHAPTER 2 – OUR CITY

I want to advocate for our citizens. This is so that our elected representatives change the way the city operates. We have inefficient management, a decaying infrastructure, exorbitant tax rates, and pervasive homelessness. I want to help maximize the ingenuity of each of our citizens and their potential. Philadelphia is the 5th largest city in the United States and exceptionally diverse. Although the crime rate overall has decreased since Mayor

A NEW BEGINNING

Nutter's tenure, we should not have an exceptionally high rate of homelessness, and the handling of the city budget exacerbated the situation. As a middle-class citizen, I value the dollar and what it means to each of us. I will be a staunch advocate for the poor. Taxpayers work too hard and tirelessly for it to simply vanish. In 2018, the city lost $33 million in taxpayer money possibly due to fraud. Mr. Kenney kept spiking property taxes and instated the once controversial soda tax. The citizens of Philadelphia experienced substantial rises in tax rates. I desire to help

A NEW BEGINNING

bring back the opportunity and promise that the city should provide to all Philadelphians, a comfort that the leader can be trusted in managing all aspects. We must have a plan and vision for the future. Our children need a strong education that will prepare them for life as productive citizens, crime held low, roads repaired, the environment protected, immigrants welcomed, access to affordable healthcare, and our economy stimulated so that our people can get proper employment. These can only be accomplished with the frame of mind that we can do this together and someone who is able to implement solutions to those problems. These problems do not need to exist for much longer since they can be solved effectively. I plan to delve further into the issues in the subsequent chapters.

CHAPTER 3 – EDUCATION

Education is one of the fundamental cornerstones that should be protected and expanded. More recently, our public-school system has been devastated by a massive lack of funding, a $383 million funding shortfall.

A NEW BEGINNING

This is largely a result of state underinvestment over decades. Our school district struggles to keep up with standards and demands of the future. Not only has the public-school system been dwindling, but the entirety of parochial schools has also decreased since the 1990s. We've witnessed multiple mergers and closures. Since private schools are not affiliated with the city of Philadelphia, they must be funded by the community. We should not ignore that we do have an existing education crisis. I am an ardent supporter of public education. Our

A NEW BEGINNING

standards lag other cities nationwide. The city should focus on revitalizing our schools. School choice is an option desired by many parents who believe the public school system does not meet their needs in Philadelphia. I support the recommendations of the Healthy Philly Schools Initiative and a firm believer in the Common Core standards initiative. The CCSI states that there should be a national base standard for schools to meet specific criteria. Each student should receive instruction on an individualized basis and standardized testing must be discouraged. By

A NEW BEGINNING

each grade level, students must meet requisite

requirements to move onto the next grade. If

we ignore each pupil's gifts, we cannot

measure their achievements. I also believe

that teachers must be granted enough pay and

that their rights must remain intact. Labor

laws should protect teachers who choose to

strike due to low wages. The goal for our

children is for them to become informed and

productive citizens in our society and be able

to contribute to its overall betterment. They

are unable to accomplish this if they

experience a lack of foundation in their

A NEW BEGINNING

intellectual development. We must increase funding for education, so that schools can attain the resources they need such as school supplies, improved capital, and infrastructure to provide for the needs of our city's students. Mayor Kenney's proposed solution to the problem of underfunded pre-K education was to instate a soda tax upon Philadelphians. I will discuss the soda tax in more detail in Chapter 5: The Economy. Kenney desired pre-K education to be universal and it cost upwards of $40 million. While local control of the Philadelphia School District can be

A NEW BEGINNING

beneficial, new methods of funding schools must be explored. Charter schools are categorized as businesses that survive independently, rather than the state-run public-school system. We must focus on improved technical and vocational programs, and for those seeking a college education we need to equip them with the tools they need. Our children are the future of Philadelphia and in caring for them we make a better tomorrow possible for all of us. Philadelphia must provide for its intellectual talent and instill its growth in all the young people in the

A NEW BEGINNING

city. I am a testament and the exemplification of that fact that all citizens can achieve the pinnacle of knowledge. Knowledge is essential and is an effective tool for gaining skills by direct observation and can be best utilized for job training. Job training provides our people with the ability to conduct their duties in employment and through workshops these skills can be maintained. Our children can reach their fullest heights through educational reform so that they may maintain the promise of our tomorrow.

CHAPTER 4: CRIME

Crime is defined as an offensive act against another person or their property prohibited by law. Law defines these types of acts as *mala in se* and *mala prohibita*. *Mala in se* acts are inherently evil such as murder, while *mala prohibita* outlines practices that are not necessarily illegal but are regulated such as parking in a prohibited area. It often originates from a variety of environmental, social, and cognitive factors. Firstly, those without a role model are more likely to

A NEW BEGINNING

commit crimes and those who live in predisposed neighborhoods are more likely to participate. This does not mean just because a specific race lives in an area means that they are all criminals. We must avoid generalizations and having preconceived notions that will taint our perspectives of the world. However, cities can take precautionary measures to reduce crime. These measures include neighborhood surveillance, improving the police's relations with the community, and community activities. The more that the people recognize

A NEW BEGINNING

that police are meant to protect and keep them

from harm, the more they will realize they are

on their side. Excessive policing can often

send the wrong message to communities, and

the people believe they can't be trusted to act

properly. This can be avoided by having

better interactions with our police and

neighborhoods. Crime has significantly

decreased under Mayor Kenney, hitting a 40-

year low in 2016. I believe that crime

originates from a lack of information and

education. If our kids feel as if they aren't

performing well in school, they can resort to

A NEW BEGINNING

acting out and embroiling themselves into trouble. A method through which neighborhoods can curtail crime is to instate more after-school and neighborhood activities that provide a productive outlet for passing the time. This will prevent kids from entering gang related violence or becoming a victim of a homicide. Community policing can be effective through the police forming bonds with the community instead of them being threats. After the case *Terry v. Ohio*, police officers were granted more discretion

A NEW BEGINNING

in conducting a search and expanded the notion of reasonable suspicion.

As for my position on addressing crime, I tend to favor the due process model rather than crime control for citizens to feel comfortable in their communities. However, if violent crime becomes rampant, we must take the proper measures to ensure that we keep our people safe and instate harsher penalties.

At this juncture, there is a growing debate about the role of weapons in our

A NEW BEGINNING

society. Due to our inherent 2nd amendment right, guns cannot simply be banned. I believe that the Founding Fathers intended that we all have the right to defend ourselves from an oppressive government. Gun control can be effective in some cases. If we enact stricter gun control laws in urban areas, this can be counterproductive. This is due to criminals gaining access to weapons through other means such as the black market or illegal sales. In the city of Philadelphia, while I do not support banning handguns or rifles, I do support an assault weapons ban as there

A NEW BEGINNING

should be no need for such a weapon to be utilized on city grounds. I support concealed carry being banned within the city as well as making open carry permissible. I also support increased background checks to gain more insight into individuals who wish to purchase a weapon. If they have a mental illness or a prior criminal history, they should not be granted access to a weapon. This does not violate due process as the proper measures have been taken to confirm the irrefutable fact that a person is not deemed fit to carry a weapon in their possession. An important

A NEW BEGINNING

part of preventing crime is treating those with mental illnesses, which serves as the underlying issue. Many of the gun related crimes that were perpetrated in the United States such as Adam Lanza in Connecticut and Nikolas Cruz in Florida involved those with a serious mental illness that was not properly addressed. Our mental health care system must be upgraded and have increased resources to recognize those who are exhibiting signs of destructive behaviors. To protect our citizens from violent crimes, we need to improve measures to recognize when

A NEW BEGINNING

someone is acting out of the ordinary and exhibiting erratic behaviors. This will allow us enough time to respond and report those individuals to authorities. If we accomplish this, we can avoid tragedies that are becoming more commonplace.

A more controversial action to prevent crime is deterrence. By deterring criminals with policing and capital punishment, it may reduce crime in the short term but will have little effect in the long term. While our prisons are becoming overcrowded, a potential solution to this problem is criminal

A NEW BEGINNING

rehabilitation. Rehabilitating criminals after they commit crimes is the best way to allow non-violent offenders to become reintegrated into society. By choosing to release prisoners after an extended period of community service, skill building, job training, and correcting erroneous behaviors, they can return to their lives after a transformative experience. Once they return to society, they will have a decreased incidence of crimes and run-ins with the law. In my opinion, this is the best method to solve the overcrowding of our prisons in the city. As for capital punishment,

A NEW BEGINNING

I oppose the death penalty in all cases. I do not believe that it is the right of the state to take someone else's life for any perceived justifiable reasons. All life should be respected, and people should be given a second chance to correct their mistakes, this can be done through their punishment for wrongdoings.

On the issue of terrorism and security, there have been rampant attacks throughout the world and in the United States. Measures should be sought to prevent a tragedy from occurring such as relaying information to the

A NEW BEGINNING

proper authorities. As citizens, the best course of action is to report individuals who may pose a threat in the community. I do believe that the right to privacy is important, and that all citizens are entitled to civil liberties, but we must do whatever means necessary to protect our people from external and internal dangers.

Another major causative factor for crime is the lack of opportunity and poor urban planning. When economic opportunities do not exist such as viable employment or being forced to live in

A NEW BEGINNING

poverty, there often seems like there can be no hope. Due to a lack of hope, citizens resort to violence since they feel left out of their communities, which can be the explanation for erratic behaviors. By restoring this hope through more affordable housing, access to job training and employment, we can allow our citizens to feel the true promise of Philadelphia. And instead of choosing crime, they will choose contribution which will be rewarded. Better urban planning can benefit our city exponentially through finding specific focal points for activity centers, allowing local businesses to grow in poverty-stricken communities. We should be building more grocery stores and shopping centers in these areas for citizens to be granted access to much needed resources. The problem of crime originates from a lack of resources, and it can be so severe that people resort to killing each other. This is unacceptable, and with better urban planning, more resources, and equal opportunity we are better able to live in harmony with one another.

CHAPTER 5: THE ECONOMY

A NEW BEGINNING

The economy is one of the most important areas of public policy that cannot be ignored. There are multiple factors which affect individual citizens like us, businesses, and the government. These factors are inflation, unemployment, and wages. When prices are too high, citizens and their paychecks cannot adequately keep pace with them. Unemployment affects us and businesses by not being able to support our families and an inability to produce goods. This creates something known as deflation, which is considered negative growth in the

A NEW BEGINNING

economy and can spiral it into a recession. I

believe that it is the government's

responsibility to intervene in a recession if

the business cycle does not immediately

resolve it. This can prevent severe

repercussive effects from occurring and

avoid more serious tumultuous periods

known as depressions. In the case of market

failure, the government must do whatever

means necessary to provide for the survival

of a free market system. Market failures do

occur by externalities, which is an unwanted

byproduct. I will talk more about externalities in a later chapter.

As for Mayor Kenney's soda tax, the effects were devastating upon local businesses in the beverage industries and it affects consumers drastically as well. Any time that a price control is imposed, it decreases total surplus both for the producer and consumer. The free market should not be interfered with due to destabilizing supply and demand. Due to a decrease in demand for soda due to a new soda tax, consumers will choose to buy fewer soft drinks and thus

A NEW BEGINNING

revenue declines for the entire industry.

Local businesses are hurt by increased taxes,

and the tax does not fully accomplish its goal.

The tax has been criticized from both sides of

the aisle. I prefer taxes to be lowered for

working class people, and compensate for the

decreased revenue by cutting spending in

other non-essential areas. Despite this, I

believe vital areas such as healthcare and

education should not receive cuts to funding.

I believe that these must remain intact to

preserve essential services for each of our

citizens. By curbing spending, we keep the

deficit manageable and not allow our city to become entrenched in debt. Creating more jobs is important so that citizens can be granted access to more opportunity. Programs that provide aid such as Medicaid must not be modified because those who live in poverty need extra support for living assistance.

Earlier in 2018, the city of Philadelphia reportedly lost $33 million in taxpayer revenue attributed to fraud. I believe that to be more transparent, the public must know where their hard-earned funds are going.

A NEW BEGINNING

While this responsibility is solely delegated to the city controller, the executive can take actions to reduce corruption in government. Those who are suspected to exploit the system and pose a risk to taxpayer funding should be removed from their positions as soon as possible. Our citizens cannot afford to have their money squandered since this funding would have gone toward projects to benefit the public. Corruption is a pervasive problem, and it must be controlled or else our government will be wasteful and inefficient.

A NEW BEGINNING

We cannot settle for anything less than transparency from government officials.

A plan to create jobs is simple. We need to invest in job training for our youth and equip them with the skills and education they need to succeed. Another method by which we create jobs is by stimulating the local economy. This is through establishing more recreational and dining areas, building more parks, and bringing shopping centers and recreational facilities to neighborhoods. By lowering taxes, we will attract a greater number of restaurants and businesses while

A NEW BEGINNING

granting an incentive for them to conduct financial transactions. These should be top priorities to encourage growth in our city and granting more options for those in poorer communities by providing funding to build more local grocery stores and improving infrastructure. Encouraging more public works projects such as new development projects for housing, rebuilding our roads and schools, and investing more in our capital to make productivity even more efficient.

B businesses will be more likely to increase wages and grant bonuses to their

A NEW BEGINNING

employees due to extra revenue. I am a proponent of raising the minimum wage relative to inflation. While raising the wage is detrimental to businesses in the short term, it is beneficial to employees in the long term. If the minimum wage were raised high too quickly, new employees could not be hired, leading to greater unemployment. This is counterproductive, as businesses rely on the greatest number of employees at the lowest cost. Employees would see the greatest benefits originating from raises. Another prominent issue is that of economic

A NEW BEGINNING

inequality for women and minorities. Philadelphia, a major U.S. city, must be a beacon of light. We all are unique and have something to contribute to our society. Knowing this, we should enforce laws and regulations to prevent discrimination in the workplace as it is illegal to pay someone less based on their gender or race. It is essential to protect the interests of women and minorities on the basis that it is morally wrong and inexplicable to allow our own preconceived notions to deny opportunity based on religious affiliation, gender, color, creed, or

A NEW BEGINNING

nationality. All people deserve paid family and maternity leave, as it is their right. As for labor unions, collective bargaining rights need to remain intact and that it is an employee's right to protest their employers in a responsible manner to express their opinions. It is not permissible to take away workers' rights without a cause. Labor unions can be both beneficial and detrimental to businesses by providing more insight about their employment situations as it pertains to wages, and it can worsen the relationship between the employer and employees.

A NEW BEGINNING

Our economy is the most important aspect of our livelihood in the city of Philadelphia. Each person must be granted equal opportunity to succeed in the economy. As leaders, we provide a nationwide example of how we treat our own citizens and provide for their own individual wealth. It will lead to improved rewards in the workplace, and we can harness it to achieve greater things for our city. By cutting taxes and excessive regulations, growing commerce, providing suitable housing for the poor, preventing corruption and discrimination, and encouraging public works projects, we can truly experience the fullest of our potential by embracing the vitality it brings to our city.

CHAPTER 6: IMMIGRATION

The executive order signed by President Trump in 2017 to ban immigration from Muslim countries. Depending on your point of view, this action can be interpreted as either discriminatory or as protecting our security. We are all a nation of immigrants and should be proud of this fact. Since the 1900s, millions of Americans have

A NEW BEGINNING

immigrated into the United States to seek a new promise for themselves and their families. During the 20th century, my ancestors came to this country from Italy to find opportunity and a better life. I emphasize intergenerational upward mobility, which is the ability for the family to continually improve its economic and educational standing throughout the generations. I accomplished this as the first person in my immediate family to attend college and attain a college degree.

A NEW BEGINNING

Immigrants have much to offer to our communities with high skilled labor. While it can be argued that immigrants taking lower skilled jobs can hurt American workers, our economy works best with all involved. Holding a holistic view of immigration by increasing the number of work visas is important, but at the same time being cautious about those who enter our city. I am also a proponent of amnesty and citizenship for immigrants who happen to be in our country illegally. There are currently 11 million DACA recipients in the United

A NEW BEGINNING

States. The treatment of immigrants at the U.S.-Mexico border cannot be more unsettling and heart breaking. There are law-abiding citizens who reside in our country, and witness their families be torn apart simply because they are here illegally. This ignores a facet of our society that we must be inclusive of all people. Once we can be certain of their intentions for our nation and our city, we can choose whether to admit them. If immigrants come to our city with the intent that they will further its mission and contribute to its productivity and betterment,

A NEW BEGINNING

we should allow them into our society. However, if it is found that they may pose a grave threat to our security, we cannot. Our identity depends on uniting together with people of all different races to accomplish a common goal which is the preservation of liberty and pursuit of prosperity for our citizens. We should not be afraid and condemn those who do not look or speak like us, but rather welcome them into our company and allow them to experience the fullest of the promise that our city brings.

A NEW BEGINNING

As for the sanctuary city policy, it is important to be vigilant about a small minority of immigrants who can pose a potential danger to our communities. However, we must also be holistic of those who are in our city to seek refuge. A Center for American Progress report found that sanctuary cities have lower crime rates, and they have little effect on crime. Mayor Kenney supports this policy, and I join with him in praising it. However, we must not partake in divisive rhetoric that can jeopardize our relationship with federal

A NEW BEGINNING

officials. There needs to be a compromise regarding federal grants and status of immigrants. It can be argued that those who are accused of minor crimes should not be deported. However, those who commit a felony or pose a significant risk to our citizens, be sent back to their country. Most immigrants are law-abiding citizens who pay taxes and serve their communities to their utmost abilities. These individuals should experience the fullest extent of individual liberty, opportunity, and freedom in our city.

A NEW BEGINNING

Having a multicultural and pluralistic society is important due to accommodating different cultures, traditions, and practices. Assimilationists seek to forcibly convert immigrants immediately into the American way of life. Assimilation should be a gradual process once the immigrant community becomes familiar with our customs. It is important that a culture's language is kept but that they also learn English so that they can communicate with other citizens and each other. This process forges a city that is

A NEW BEGINNING

holistic and tolerant of others' beliefs, backgrounds, and faiths.

Immigration is one of the most critical issues to the American public today. Whether you support stricter immigration policies that contribute to the welfare and benefit the well-being of our citizens, or if you are for a holistic approach to immigration, we all are immigrants of our beloved country. We are known as the "melting pot"; we assimilate and together we contribute to a common culture. We establish one national identity as Americans, and pledge allegiance to one flag

A NEW BEGINNING

and are united under God. We must set aside

our differences and find common ground in

our culture and history. Many immigrants

come to our country for the promise of the

American dream, and they deserve to

experience it fully. They are entitled to the

privileges of the American way of life and

must choose to adopt its culture and values.

This cultivates a sense of pride, and we need

to recognize those that are forgotten in our

society. When we enforce our immigration

policies, we are ensuring the safety of

American citizens in our country by

A NEW BEGINNING

preventing dangerous individuals from entering, while encouraging immigrants to enter legally. In accomplishing this, America can accommodate those who choose to be law abiding citizens and contribute to the betterment of society. However, we should not discriminate against immigrants using generalizations, but we must be wary of those we choose to allow to enter. The safety and security of our citizens must be at the forefront of our interests, while reforming immigration policies to allow easier access for immigrants and preventing those who wish to do harm from entry, will have the most beneficial effect for everyone. Society cannot function without laws, and we need to mitigate it by having sensible immigration policies, which is the ultimate solution to that crucial issue.

CHAPTER 7: SOCIAL POLICY

The aspects of social policy I will discuss in this chapter include marijuana, abortion, LGBT rights, and same-sex marriage within in the United States. I will provide factual background and my proposed

A NEW BEGINNING

solutions to these problems that face the

nation and our city. I will first begin with the

issue of abortion and its debate. In 1973, *Roe*

v. Wade was a contentious court case brought

by the plaintiff Jane Roe, against Dallas

District Attorney Henry Wade about the lack

of women's access to abortion procedures.

The Supreme Court found that under the Due

Process Clause of the 14th Amendment, that

women have the right to privacy and

autonomy to do what they choose with their

bodies. It protects their decision to have an

abortion if they choose, but this is limited to

before the third trimester of pregnancy. As a

Catholic, I believe that this issue is sensitive.

However, I support current law in

Pennsylvania. We should not penalize

women who seek an abortion or make them

face criminal charges for murder. In the event

of a danger to the child or mother's life, it is

at the discretion of the physician to determine

if the practice is deemed acceptable to

preserve both of their lives. Even in cases

when the child will likely be born with a life-

threatening defect or illness, we all should be

given a chance to live our own lives and the

child may exceed expectations. Abortion is a contentious issue, and while circumstances may differ, the law must have a uniform approach to treat each individual case with compassion and consider the interests of the woman and her circumstances.

In 2014, a monumental case titled *Obergefell v. Hodges* reached the U.S. Supreme Court. This case dealt with the ability of a same sex couple to marry under the 14th Amendment of the U.S. Constitution. It was of great national importance due to its prominence within the LGBT community.

A NEW BEGINNING

Same-sex marriage is now legal and recognized in the entirety of the United States. I wholeheartedly support this decision and for equal adoption rights for same-sex couples. It is their right to choose who their partner should be without government's interference in their personal lives. This is dependent upon the democratic ideals we were founded upon, and we must retain this freedom unabridged by any government actions. Discrimination has become a rampant issue in our country, and I support having anti-discrimination laws for those

A NEW BEGINNING

who feel that their rights are being violated due to their sexual orientation. Each person is supposed to be treated equally regardless of their orientation. If we deny equality based on any factors, we are denying our citizens the pursuit of liberty and happiness and this cannot be maintained.

Next, I'd like to focus on the issue of marijuana. In 2014, Mayor Michael Nutter introduced legislation to decriminalize 30 grams of marijuana through the Small Amount of Marijuana program (SAM). This allowed those caught with possession of

A NEW BEGINNING

marijuana to pay a fine and complete community service. This keeps people from being arrested for non-violent drug possessions. The police should shift their focus to harder drugs and addressing criminal activity related to them. Marijuana is still outlawed federally according to the Controlled Substance Act and in Pennsylvania. Local ordinances relating to marijuana but not yet seek its expansion to recreational use until there is action by the state legislature. After action by the state legislature, local laws must expand

A NEW BEGINNING

marijuana's recreational use. Conflicting state and local laws lead to discrepancies and inconsistencies with penalties. However, marijuana would be an abundant source of tax revenue to utilize for our citizens in the same regard as tobacco products. As a result, offenders simply caught with marijuana possession would be released. In 2016, Pennsylvania became the 24th state to legalize medical marijuana. More commonly, patients are treated with medical marijuana for any debilitating conditions. Marijuana can have a therapeutic effect on those suffering from

A NEW BEGINNING

illnesses and it can enhance their quality of life and recovery. While I am open to the legalization of recreational marijuana, we must be very cautious regarding the legalization of other drugs. With any drug, especially nicotine, there is a chance for substance abuse. Marijuana has also gotten a reputation for being a gateway drug and could possibly exacerbate the existing opioid crisis. I feel that substance abuse shouldn't be a criminal issue, but rather an addiction. In this case, there must be rehabilitation to prevent this addiction from spiraling out of control. In contrast, if the substance abuse is occurring in accordance with illegal activities, it should be considered related to crime and controlled properly.

CHAPTER 8: HEALTHCARE

This leads to our next topic, which is the rampant opioid crisis transpiring across our country. Because of the crisis, 72,000 Americans died due to overdose on drugs. The crisis was caused essentially by a fatalistic response due to a loss of jobs and that there was no hope to be found. Despair

A NEW BEGINNING

had set in, and citizens turned to drugs. States

such as Vermont, New Hampshire, and

Virginia experienced the worst effects of the

opioid epidemic. Apparently, doctors were

incentivizing patients to take prescription

drugs to reduce pain. However, doctors were

told to promote them by the pharmaceutical

industry. Perdue Company, the company

which produced the drug, was sued by

Pennsylvania Attorney General Josh Shapiro

due to misleading information about the

drugs. Perdue Company marketed them as

non-addictive, but in fact knew it would lead

A NEW BEGINNING

to addiction and death. Consequently, they

hold legal responsibility for the damage and

devastation they caused to so many lives.

There have been significant national and state

actions relating to the crisis to conduct

damage control. President Trump declared a

"public health emergency" in 2017. The

addiction often begins with prescription

medication and painkillers to reduce

discomfort. Patients feel the need to

continuously take the medication and become

dependent upon it. The government must

intervene to protect patients. Depending on

A NEW BEGINNING

an individual's tolerance, it can be likely that someone will develop a dependency.

There are a variety of techniques to reduce the grave threat and mortality risk that people face in their addictions. One example is the promotion of addiction treatment centers, counseling for conditions, and finding suitable housing for those afflicted. The opioid crisis has caused much devastation and suffering for families affected by it. One of the best ways to counteract the crisis is by promoting awareness and preventing patients from

A NEW BEGINNING

becoming addicted to prescription drugs. If we can make our citizens more aware that people are suffering from addictions and that this has become an epidemic, many more lives can be saved. An individual's family can also help them to rehabilitation. Rehabilitation will promote a speedy recovery and avoid addiction from becoming fatal. Pharmaceutical companies must provide medications that are non-addictive, and patients should rely on these medications to recover. Painkillers have become tremendously dangerous to our citizens and

A NEW BEGINNING

become subject to abuse. This event has often occurred inadvertently due to the high dependency risk. Overdose reversal medications must have widespread use to counteract its effects. Families should not endure suffering any longer, and more pressure must be placed on pharmaceutical companies to manufacture drugs that do not have a high addiction rate. Saving many lives by promoting rehabilitation and resources is crucial to reversing this epidemic.

Our next topic is the Patient Protection and Affordable Care Act, also known as

Obamacare. This legislation was signed into law by President Barack Obama in 2010. The law covers those with pre-existing conditions, requires you to purchase health insurance, and expands Medicare. Premiums have skyrocketed since the legislation was first implemented, and this has placed an unnecessary burden upon patients. While I do believe Obamacare is effective, I am in favor of the expansion of the increased Medicare and Medicaid provisions it grants to our elderly, disabled, and those with economic hardship. It covers the existing medical costs

A NEW BEGINNING

for these groups for them to have optimal access to healthcare.

Pharmaceutical prices in the United States have been exponentially increasing, and this is due to pharmaceutical companies monopolizing the industry and charging an unfair price to consumers in comparison to its cost of production. A life-saving drug can be exorbitantly priced on the market but costs less than one dollar to produce. These price hikes undermine our citizens and place them at risk of death if they cannot afford the drugs. The government must have a proactive role in regulating the prices of the drugs to ensure that consumers are not being treated unfairly. There must be enough access to them by mandating that pharmaceutical companies market the drugs at a reasonable price.

Chapter 9: The Environment

The environment must be protected for our posterity. It is very important that the government accounts for our natural resources and ensures that they are safeguarded. Balancing the need for energy

A NEW BEGINNING

independence and sufficiency with sensible

solutions is paramount. Supplementing

natural gas and oil with alternative energy

technologies can be a prudent way to

sustainable energy solutions for the future.

Fossil fuels will substantially decline by

2050, and there needs to be other energy

sources available. An important policy, in my

opinion, is the use of environmental policy in

the United States. Environmental policy is

constructed and enacted by an executive

administration (The President) and a federal

agency known as the EPA (Environmental

A NEW BEGINNING

Protection Agency). The EPA enforces, regulates, and proposes new laws of environmental policy. Environmental policy benefits us immensely in many ways. The laws involve CO2 emissions and implement a carbon tax to lessen the use of fossil fuels. These fossil fuels harm the environment in many ways, such as creating a greenhouse effect. The greenhouse effect traps the sun's energy in Earth's atmosphere due to the rays emitted from its surface. The greenhouse effect causes the planet to warm and creates the phenomenon of climate change.

A NEW BEGINNING

Historically, the U.S. has become dependent on fossil fuels from other nations, and this prevents the U.S. from being on a path to energy independence. Fossil fuels have a limited capacity and time frame for their use and eventually will become depleted. Fracking is a method that injects water at a high pressure into non-porous rocks to extract oil or natural gas. This method requires more scientific research, however, there are instances of earthquakes in areas such as the Midwest that have overused hydraulic fracking. Thus, we must find newer

A NEW BEGINNING

sustainable energy sources such as wind, solar, and hydroelectric energy. We are still using fossil fuels that will be exhausted. Our cars, machinery, and other means of transportation utilize this type of power, and a transition to these alternative sources of energy is necessary in the future. We must do what is best for our families and the environment.

The U.S. is currently dependent on other foreign nations such as Saudi Arabia for oil, and when there is a scarce amount of oil, prices increase. To counteract this, we use

A NEW BEGINNING

hydraulic fracking in the mainland or on the coastlines to extract oil. Hydraulic fracking is a method that has not been sufficiently scientifically tested, and its effects on the environment are unclear. Fracking is the injection of high-pressured water into non-porous rocks with the intent of extracting oil. When the water is injected, it destroys the rock, and since it is non-porous it cannot absorb any of the water. The remaining rock is left with a crack, and the oil is extracted. This can have many effects such as oil being dispersed into the surrounding area. It can

A NEW BEGINNING

seep from the oil rig or wells into the ocean or onto land. Despite the economic advantages of this process, fracking creates environmental issues. When the oil seeps into the ocean it can affect organisms, and harm or kill them. Seeping oil caused by fracking impacts the biodiversity of an ocean or a landscape. It changes many aspects of the ecosystem. It also can create earthquakes due to crack formations left behind in the rock. Fracking can also pollute the groundwater and harm peoples' health by oil seeping into pores in the soil and travelling as runoff. This

A NEW BEGINNING

is the reason the use of fracking should be discouraged in populated areas, near wildlife, or conservation areas. Subsidies should be given for other sources of energy such as solar or wind power. I support fracking in areas with low population density after extensive scientific testing. Solar and wind power are sustainable measures to combat climate change and are natural methods of powering communities. These methods cannot be used on their own, however, due to the Sun not always shining or the wind always blowing. Communities need power

A NEW BEGINNING

constantly and this cannot be accomplished solely on wind and solar energy. There must be a supplement to these methods such as natural gas. Natural gas is more efficient and can be accessed in other means instead of fracking such as synthetic natural gas.

The United States' energy sources mainly consist of coal and fossil fuels. These sources are non-renewable which means that there is a limited capacity and are expected to run out. These sources of energy are known to contribute to global climate change. Climate change is a natural phenomenon that

A NEW BEGINNING

needs to be addressed by our government. The production and release of CO2 and Methane causes global warming, the rise of temperatures in our planet. These can cause the sun's rays to radiate more intensely on the Earth's atmosphere and for the polar ice caps to melt. This results in a rising sea level that has the potential to create tsunamis in certain places such as Florida. We must be on a path to alternative and sustainable energy sources. This is a gradual process that occurs over a certain period. Fossil fuels will run out in less than 100 years, and wind, solar, nuclear, and hydroelectric power are sources that need investment. By using these power sources, carbon emissions will be reduced, and climate change will be halted. Until new technologies are available and affordable, the U.S. should continue its current path. The transition away from coal and fossil fuels must begin. Coal should be replaced with natural gas and supplemented with other energy sources such as wind, solar, and hydroelectric power. Wind power is harnessed by turbines, solar power can be utilized from solar panels, and hydroelectric power is generated from dams. These sources generate little or no emissions, which is conducive to a productive, healthy environment and a healthy life. By advocating for alternative and sustainable energy sources, providing tax credits to wind and solar industry, and moving toward a path of energy independence, the U.S. can use its capabilities to serve in the best interest of its people and provide for their welfare.

Chapter 10: Conclusion

A NEW BEGINNING

As I provide you with final thoughts, I'd like you to think critically about your surroundings within your city. What positive change and impact will you make into the future? Whether we choose to become involved in our communities supporting local businesses or nonprofits, or if we desire to advocate for political causes, we must feel free to do so to advocate for change. The impact of our efforts will vary, and our motivation will be questioned. We must strive to make contributions and encourage productive dialogue on many of the prevalent

A NEW BEGINNING

public policy issues. Problems should not be

left unsolved, and everyone has something to

offer for a solution. It is important to

recognize the circumstances surrounding the

issues that arise and develop pertinent

solutions to address those problems. If

effective solutions are devised, it will

improve the quality of life of everyday

citizens. An ideal city cannot be forged

without proactive engagement of its people. I

am grateful to have provided you with my

own stances and an overview surrounding

these issues. I sincerely hope it will allow you

A NEW BEGINNING

to define your own. Fixing society's

problems will ultimately make it better and

that should be our goal.

www.ingramcontent.com/pod-product-compliance
Lightning Source LLC
Chambersburg PA
CBHW020327290526
45785CB00007B/2947